MW01257943

# Through it ALL

## GAIL ESTELLA

www.TrueVinePublishing.org

Through It All
Gail Estella

Published by
True Vine Publishing Co
810 Dominican Dr. Ste 103
Nashville, TN 37228
www.TrueVinePublishing.org

ISBN: 978-1-962783-36-1 Paperback
ISBN: 978-1-962783-37-8 eBook

Printed in the United States—First Printing

# DEDICATION

This book is dedicated to family, friends, clients, and mentors that encouraged, loved, and saw something in me that I wasn't always able to see in myself. I say thank you!

# ACKNOWLEDGEMENTS

Thank you God for being God. Thank you for delivering and saving me. Your grace and mercy has given me a second chance at life. For this I will continue to honor, love and serve You.

To my mother, Lottie J. Wright, who helped to save my life. I was that lost sheep, and even though she had two more children she used her love and courageousness to rescue me.

To my father, Willie L. Wright, the provider, protector, and rock of our family. Thank you for allowing God to change you into the husband, father, and grandfather who loves and will do anything for his family. You are a true man of God.

To my sisters, Debra Wright and Moronda Ifill. Thank you for loving me "Through it all." I am eternally filled with love and gratitude to you.

To my husband, Roddey Fair. Your love for me makes me happy. You have accepted me and my past. This allows me to be free to be myself with you. For this, I am truly grateful. I love you!

And last but not least, thank you to my beautiful daughter Asja' Alexanderia McCullough. God prepared me to be your mother. You are the best thing that I ever did. Thank you for showing me what patience, hope, trust, perseverance, and faith in God truly looked like. Thank you for loving me unconditionally. Your death has caused me to live. Until we meet again my sweet, sweet Asja'. Mommy loves you more and more with each passing day. 2 Samuel 12:23

# TABLE OF CONTENTS

# INTRODUCTION

*W*omen around the world are suffering and enduring the hardships of life in silence. Some hardships are brought on by unforeseen circumstances, while others can be self-inflicted due to our own low self-esteem, lack of judgment, and poor decision-making. I've come to believe that nothing we go through is ever wasted. Every stumble, every setback, they're all lessons in disguise, teaching us and helping us guide others away from the same pitfalls.

Throughout my journey, I was able to pinpoint insecurity as the root of many of the bad decisions and wrong turns in my life. The more I listened to the experiences of other women, the more it became clear to me a long time ago that insecurity was the culprit for the hardship, hurt, and pain in many women's lives.

I wrote this book for two very simple reasons. One is to help women who are where I once was feel empowered and know that they are overcomers. There always victory awaiting those who don't give up the fight. The other is to share the depths of insecurity and how vital it is that we know who we are and who's we are.

In a world where everyone's always comparing themselves to each other and chasing this impossible idea of perfection, it's easy to lose sight of who we really are. Trust me, I've been there, done that, and got the T-shirt. And now? Well, now I'm sharing my story in the hopes that you might find something in it—something real, relatable, and maybe even life-changing. Allow my struggles to become your lessons, and allow my lessons to become your liberty

CHAPTER ONE:

# INSECURITIES

*"There is no such thing as perfect security, only varying levels of insecurity."*

—*Salman Rushdie*

*We* all have a place, a person, or an event that shapes our lives somehow. For me, I was in the sixth grade and it was Fairwold Middle School in Columbia, South Carolina. Have you ever looked around a place, noticing that there was something different about those around you? Whether good or bad. Sometimes, those differences can be legitimate; other times, they can be preconceived notions based on our own ideologies about who we are and how we view ourselves.

My time at Fairwold Middle School brought me face-to-face with insecurity. It was the first time that I can remember comparing myself. On the first day of school, I began to look at the other girls and take intel of what was different about them. The noticeable difference was boyfriends. There were no boyfriends in elementary school. It wasn't even a thought that crossed my mind. But here I was, staring up a hill at a group of light-skinned girls with long hair and their boyfriends. In a split second, before I could even look away, I began to feel ugly.

Although our skin complexions were the same, there was something different between them and me. Was it their long hair or the fact that they had boyfriends that made me feel ugly? I don't know, but I knew that when I looked at them, I felt like I didn't measure up, that I wasn't attractive, and that something about them made me feel inferior.

Middle school was a tough time for me. Everything that happened just made me feel even more unsure of myself. My school memories are filled with moments that make me cringe, like when I felt rejected and faced embarrassing failures. I recall getting kicked out of the school chorus because I wasn't a great singer. I also remember constantly feeling self-conscious about my body shape; I was slim on top but had wide hips. My shape made me self-conscious because I thought it brought unwarranted attention from boys. I dreaded sleepovers at my friend's houses. I hated walking to the community center in my neighborhood because the boys would watch us pass by. I don't know if it was because I was shy, uncomfortable, or insecure, but whatever it was, it made me feel uneasy.

If I didn't already feel bad enough about myself, there was one day that solidified my low self-esteem. I was in the car with friends, and my friend's nephew decided to weigh in on everyone's looks. "You're pretty, you're pretty," and then, looking me in the face, there was a resounding silence. He didn't call me pretty, he didn't call me ugly, he didn't say anything at all. But his lack of affirming words rang loudly, echoing in my soul in an attempt to define and label me.

His silence felt like a sharp, rusty blade stabbing into my heart. It was the moment I came face-to-face with my insecurities. My thoughts were now staring at me and confronting me in front of everyone. I'd always believed I wasn't as pretty as the other girls, and when boys were around, that feeling became amplified. I didn't realize then how much this feeling would impact my life.

Insecurity started as a seed, as it usually does in most of us, but by the time high school started, it had become a tree that overshadowed my life. Desperate to escape the fear and insecurity I felt, I took a rebellious and unruly path. I made a lot of poor choices, from the people I dated to drinking and using marijuana. I thought I was taking control of my life and being confident by skipping class or not doing as well as I could have in school. But what I was doing was the complete opposite.

I didn't know it then, but I had subconsciously chosen to focus on all the negative thoughts I had about myself despite my great qualities and characteristics. Isn't it funny how our minds tend to hold on to the bad stuff and forget the good? Life's like a big picture, and you can choose what you want to focus on. If you always look at the not-so-great stuff, you might miss out on all the beautiful things around you. You might think, "I don't look for bad stuff. It just happens." But really, you can decide how you want to see things. The saying goes, "You can see the cup as half empty or half full." It's all about how you choose to look at it. The tricky part is that unless you train yourself to see the good, you will be drawn to the bad.

Insecurity is like a quiet voice of uncertainty that stays deep inside our thoughts, making us wonder if we're truly worthy holding us back from our aspirations. It makes us doubt what we can do and how smart we are. It tries to convince us that we're insufficient and don't merit love, achievement, or joy. But I'm here to tell you, from my own experience, that those voices are just untrue tales, and unless you decide that the truth is something different, you will continue to live in the lie.

Back in high school, I was a social butterfly. I showed up at every party and every event and had a friendly connection with just about everyone. If you met me, you'd probably think I was the most confident girl. But let's peel back the layers to see what drove my behavior.

I wasn't at every gathering because I genuinely wanted to be. I am really an introvert; I loved being out and around others, but I was okay with being alone. It all came down to one thing: I just wanted to be liked. I worried that if I missed an event, my friends might move on without me and find someone else to replace me. To be even more honest, my insecurity went so far that I believed people talked negatively about me when I wasn't there. I was projecting my feelings onto them. This was a big realization for me.

I needed the feeling of being liked and valued by someone else to find value in myself, so the idea of having a boyfriend appealed to me. It represented someone caring about me. I remember my first year in high school. The hallways were big and full of older students holding hands and being close. It made me wonder if anyone would take an interest in me. At the time, I didn't realize why it resonated so deeply with me, but once I got a little older and started to search my heart and memories for the first time, I felt the need to feel valued. I found the source.

I realized that my dad, being in the military, was a big part of it. He would be away for a long time, and when he returned, it felt like we were meeting for the first time. We had to get reacquainted all over again. Just as we were getting close, he would have to leave again. And I went through the same thing with making friends. We constantly moved around, which meant new schools, people, and places. I was always making friends only to lose them and finding myself getting adjusted to new ways of life only to be uprooted once again. This happening over and over made me want stable and lasting relationships. It showed me how my early experiences shaped my desire and the need to feel safe and connected.

But there is one massive downside to not feeling valued. Because you attract who you are and not what you want, you will likely end up with someone who doesn't value you. The one thing about fear and insecurity is that it drives your decision-making ability, which is paramount because the choices that we make can propel us to do great things, be great people, and live a great life, or our choices can take us to a place that we never thought we would go, somewhere dark, somewhere lonely, somewhere sad, just by one wrong choice.

And that's how it was for me, the one wrong choice. Having insecurities, not feeling good about myself, and not liking myself allowed me to be in situations I shouldn't have been in. I allowed myself to do things that I shouldn't have done to people please, to try to fit in with the crowd. And that kept me being this person, that person, whoever I needed to be to feel valued. Even if it wasn't real. And mostly, for some reason, I wanted to fit in with the male species—a boy. I just wanted to have a boyfriend.

I can remember going to Spring Valley High School, and I saw a person there, and he was so intriguing to me. The way he looked, his body shape, his stance, everything about him appealed to me. And I liked him, but he didn't want me. I was there with two other people, and one of the girls had a light complexion and long hair. And guess what? That's the person he liked, and those feelings of insecurity resurfaced again. We became platonic friends from that meeting, and he would often ask me about her and try to date her, but I don't think she was interested. And I just can't remember vividly how the two of us got together, but we did. There was a rumor that he had a girlfriend or his ex-girlfriend, who was his son's mother, and he was supposedly abusive to her and would stalk her.

But it wasn't a rumor. It was true, but it didn't matter to me at this time because he wasn't my boyfriend, and this wasn't going to happen to me. So, we became friends, and we became involved with each other. I liked him. But it was never a formally committed relationship. We had the type of relationship where we could be friends or be involved with each other for six months at a time, maybe three months at a time, and then, for some reason, someone would stop contacting the other person. I went out one night, and he was at a party, and after seeing him, our relationship resumed. We were off and on, but I wanted more. I wanted a committed relationship with him.

Christmas time came around, and I was wondering whether or not he was going to buy me a gift. I woke up at home on Christmas just hoping that the doorbell would ring and it would be him with a Christmas present for me. But it didn't happen, and another time for my birthday, I wanted to spend my birthday with him, and I called him and asked if he would spend my birthday with me, and he told me he didn't have any money. But that was okay for me, or at least I convinced myself it was. I paid for a hotel room that night, and I just enjoyed being with him as I thought back on our time together. When we woke up the next day, I wondered when we would see each other again.

I took our relationship for what it was because I enjoyed being with him, even though I saw signs of red flags. It wasn't a whole lot that I saw looking back when we were younger because, like I said, he had another girlfriend, and I would imagine with aggression or whatever it is that he did, it was to her and not to me, and as time moved on, I moved to Charlotte, North Carolina, and he left. He went to Kansas, and I didn't see him, so I began to have other relationships and dated other people.

I was at work one day, and my girlfriend called me and told me he was in Columbia.

Wow. I had to get there, and I did, and I remember that night seeing him, and my parents had gone out of town. I was grown now, maybe 26 or 27 years old, but those feelings were still there for him. I loved him. From the first day I met him, I loved him. And I loved him in a way that I don't think I loved anyone else.

We finally agreed to a committed relationship, and everything was good for a long time. He was intriguing and spontaneous, and we would go places and do things. I was on Cloud Nine because that's how high I felt, and then the little signs began to come. We would go out, and one night, I was ready to go, but he wasn't. I remember there being a lot of shoving. Sometimes, we would go places, and if I stayed in the car, he would say, "Don't leave me." I wondered why he would say don't leave me. Why would I have a reason to leave you? I didn't put that together until later when the first incident of domestic violence happened.

# CHAPTER TWO:

# DOMESTIC VIOLENCE

*"Domestic Abuse is an epidemic, and yet we don't properly address it. It is time for the DA to be exposed."*
—*Gail Estella*

The first time the domestic violence happened, we had gone out one night, and we had been drinking. We both worked in Charlotte and had to go to work the following day. I was ready to go home, but our disagreement turned into an argument, and the next thing I knew, he had pushed me down. He pushed me into the bushes. I felt hurt and humiliated. I couldn't believe this was happening to me. Why is this happening to me? I know he's not doing this to me, but he was doing this to me. I tried to fight back, but as a woman, I was not strong enough to defend myself. It only made things worse. Eventually, it stopped, and he pulled me up. We got in the car, I dropped him off at his mother's house, and went home.

Still in a state of shock, still numb, still disappointed, still hurt, my mind began to become flooded with questions. How could this happen? We were happy, and things were going well. Why was this happening to me? What decision do I make now? How do I make a decision right now? God, I don't want to make a decision right now. I don't want this to be happening. I just want it to be better; I want it to be like it was, and the following day, he called and told me he was sorry. He apologized.

The honeymoon stage: The honeymoon stage is the stage after abuse happens. The abuser goes to the victim and tells the victim that they're sorry. I didn't mean to do it. I don't know what happened to me. I promise, just don't leave. Please just don't leave, it'll never happen again. The honeymoon stage is when everything is fun and going well, you're enjoying each other, and it lasts for a while, but it's a repetitious cycle.

I wanted to believe that it would never happen again. He told me everything I needed to hear, and because I wanted to believe him, I went to pick him up the next morning, and we rode to Charlotte to work. I was not strong enough to let the first time be the last. The first time was the beginning of many times because I was not strong enough to walk away. Now, I know I did not love myself enough, value myself enough, and was too insecure to put myself first at that moment.

Insecurity can be a gateway to domestic violence because it can prevent you from paying attention to red flags and acknowledging the signs. You try to do things to appease others and disregard the red flags. Don't ignore the signs. They may be subtle, but they are signs, and if we pay attention to them, we can avoid toxic and abusive relationships. Insecurity causes us to stay or go back to abusive and toxic relationships where we think they have a right because we are giving silent permission when we refuse to walk away. I heard someone say that we go from being a victim to a volunteer. In the beginning, when things happen to you, you are a victim because you didn't sign up for it or ask for it. It happened against your will. But in time, you allow that person to hurt you voluntarily. We have to take ownership of our part to find the courage to walk away and heal from what has happened.

We can make excuses and reasons that sound good to us, but when the abuse gets terrible enough, we will get tired enough to decide to leave. The unfortunate part is it takes some longer to get tired than others, and some women have lost their lives because they couldn't walk away. Some people hear domestic violence and only think about the physical aspect of it, but what about emotional, psychological, sexual, or financial abuse? Isolation, intimidation, control. By the time physical contact occurs, you have already experienced other forms of abuse. I remember when people used to say that my ex used to abuse his girlfriend. I knew it was true, but I didn't think it would happen to me. His sayings, "Stay here, don't leave, or we don't need anyone else, just us," were all bright red flags I couldn't see. It can sound romantic, but it was possessive and unhealthy.

I knew that I stayed in that relationship much longer than I should have, and it was toxic. It began to drain me. It started to make me feel sad and depressed. But when there wasn't abuse, we had fun because he was so spontaneous, so vibrant, and we would go out and have such a good time. But if we were out and he was drinking, and I saw him order tequila or grand mariner, I knew it would not be a good night. After he drank, I could see the switch taking place in his eyes, and I would already know that night I was going to be abused.

One night, we went to the club, and I was wearing a pretty white suit with long earrings, and we were listening to a band. There was a member of the band who had locs in his hair, and I liked locs. After our night of fun, we hopped in my car, a Fierro, a tiny two-seater, and on the way home, I mentioned how I liked the locs of the band members' hair, and all of a sudden, out of nowhere, he said, " I told you I didn't like long earrings," and he slapped the earrings off of my ears. He deviated off the interstate and went behind a gas station, where he continued to abuse me for commenting on someone's hair.

His thing was that we were a unit and didn't need the outside. We just needed only the two of us. He often told me we would move away somewhere far, like Washington State, where it would just be the two of us. When we went out, he always wanted me to give him my undivided attention to look at only him. I'm a stylist. I'm a creative person. I like looking at people's hair, I like looking at people's shoes, I like looking at what they have on, and he always wanted me just to look at him, and we had gone out this night to this club, and I had on this beautiful sheer dress.

Initially, I didn't want him to go, but I changed my mind, and he went with me. We did well in the club that night. We danced, we talked, and it was a great time. And I guess he saw me looking at someone and pulled me outside the club. He said, come on out, and I went out, and he just tore the dress like it was a piece of paper. He just tore it off of me. Thank God I had a white Leotard underneath it. There was no physical abuse that night, but there was emotional abuse and psychological abuse.

I took him to court over what happened that night, and when we went before the judge, the judge said, "Well, did he tell you he would make restitution?" I said, "Yes, he did." And the judge replied, "Well, if he's going to make restitution, maybe we should drop the charges." Because I had never been in a situation like this before, I listened to the judge and dropped the charges. There seemed to be no way out of this. It was like the abuse wasn't real to anyone but me.

And then there was the financial abuse. One day, he came to my job and told me to go outside. Me being a cosmetologist, I got paid every day, and this was before digital forms of payment. People paid with cash, and I had a pocket full of money because I had a great clientele. As I stepped outside of the salon, he continued to pull on me, trying to force me into the alley. I remember going to the window and looking inside. It seems so animated to me now as I look back. It was as if it was happening in slow motion. One of my client's husband was in the salon at that time, and he saw me trying to cry out for help, but I would later learn that he was an abuser himself, so he didn't do anything to try to help me.

I entered the alley, and he told me to get in the car. I asked him why and told him I was working but proceeded to get in the car. Once inside the car, he took my money and kidnapped me. He took me from York County down to Chester County. He just drove me around and drove me around and drove me around. Finally, he brought me back, and I returned to work where my clients were still sitting, waiting on me. Later, he came back that night to pick me up like nothing had happened.

There were times when I would give him the money to pay the rent, which would never get paid. There was an incident when I called the maintenance people to come and take care of an issue, and they told me they couldn't come because the rent hadn't been paid in two months. Then, when I hesitated to give him money again for the rent, he questioned my trust in him. Being naive and insecure, I would give him the money, and the same thing would happen again.

All the craziness I experienced was often overshadowed by the good times when I would get out of work and be tired. We would go home, and he would run my bath water, and he would bathe me, pick me up and carry me to the bed, lotion me down, and put my pajamas on me. He would go shopping for me, and I'd get home from work, and the outfit would be lying on the bed with cologne already sprayed on him, and I would put the outfit on for the night. When times were good, they were good. And when they were terrible, they were terrible. The good times were fun, but they came with a price and the price was abuse.

I began to feel so ugly and defeated from the abuse I suffered that I could no longer look in the mirror at myself. When I went to work at the salon, there were mirrors everywhere, but I couldn't bring myself to face my reflection. I would style my clients' hair and turn them around to look at themselves, but I didn't allow myself to look at my reflection. I went to work every day looking pretty and put together with a new hairstyle every week, make-up, and beautiful clothes. The outside looked good, but the inside was so ugly.

Why am I mentioning these stories? So that you can see the different types of abuse, and so if you are in an abusive relationship and have chosen to ignore the red flags, hopefully, my own experiences can be a lens into the truth. These experiences also speak to the power of insecurity and how its firm grip on your identity can keep you in toxic, harmful, and dangerous situations.

# CHAPTER THREE:

# ADDICTION

*"The night is far gone, the day is at hand. So then let us cast off the works of darkness and put on the armor of light."*

—*Romans 13:12 (KJV)*

*D*omestic abuse wasn't the only form of abuse that I found myself in due to my insecurities. I also suffered from drug abuse. Finally, breaking things off and leaving that abusive relationship sent me reeling back into the world of substance abuse, but the habit began to form in high school. Alcohol was my first drug of choice. And I can remember maybe 15 or 16 trying alcohol for the very first time. Now that I look back on it, I overindulged; when others around me might have stopped, I just continued. I remember going to a party one night in high school and drinking until I had to throw up. I was at this clubhouse, and I went in the bathroom, and I threw up. The person who would later become my abuser just looked at me with disgust.

If it wasn't alcohol, then it was marijuana. I always thought I had to have something to offer if I went around a person. There was a guy I was dating at the time, and I felt that anytime I saw him or went around, I had to bring marijuana. I smoked marijuana. I can't say that I was addicted to marijuana. I can't even say that I was addicted to alcohol. The addictions would come later, but this is where they started. As I said before, some things begin as seeds. Not everything occurs in your life, whether negative or positive, in one moment. That is why we must be careful in our decision-making; what starts as a fun time in one season can become a full-blown addiction in another. I didn't just stop at marijuana. My first time trying cocaine, I snorted it. I liked the way it made me feel. I can't even say that I was addicted to cocaine at the time. I just knew that I enjoyed indulging in it.

In 1985, I moved to Charlotte, North Carolina, and I began to date this guy while I was there. we partied, drank, and smoked marijuana, but I didn't know that he was involved with crack cocaine. I knew what crack cocaine was, and I might have tried it before then, but if I did, it wasn't regular. There would be times when all of us would be out in the common area, and he would be in the back by himself. I didn't know what he was doing. I just knew that he would excuse himself from the rest of us.

Until one night, his friend said, "He's back there smoking that shit." I didn't know what it was, but it made me wonder what he was doing that would keep him away from everyone else. I was curious. What was it? How did it make him feel? Maybe I wanted to try it. One weekend, my friend Jennifer came up, and we were playing cards and snorting. I wanted more, and they said, "We just had a round, chill, chill." I tried to chill, but there was something inside of me that just wanted more. And I eventually got to see what it was that the person I was dating was doing. He was smoking cocaine, crack cocaine.

Back then, you had to cook crack cocaine yourself. I tried it, smoked it through a glass tube, and couldn't get it. I didn't know how. I couldn't get the feeling of what it was that they were doing. So, I just continued to snort. One of his friends came down from DC, and I was on my way to work. His friend had this apparatus that I used to try to smoke cocaine, which was the first time I felt that I got something out of smoking. And it was an immediate high for me. An instant euphoria. That was the time that I crossed that imaginary line from indulging to addiction.

I remember the feeling. I went to work, and the entire time I was there, I could only think about getting back home because I just wanted that feeling again. From that moment, my addiction took off, and it became destructive. The good thing about it for me was the fact that I worked every day. I made money every day, but it wasn't enough money for me to pay my bills because I would spend the money that I made to feed my addiction, and things began to get bad. So bad that I eventually had to move back home. I broke up with my boyfriend and moved back with my parents. I stopped using cocaine for a while, and life started to get better for me, so I moved back to Charlotte. I got an apartment, and

I could pay my bills for my apartment. This was my second chance to get things right.

It was around this time that I entered the abusive relationship that we talked about in the last chapter. While I was waiting for that relationship to get better, I needed something to numb the pain of what was happening to me. So, I went back to what I knew. I went back to the crack cocaine. I tried to hide it from him because he didn't do cocaine, but eventually, he found out, and we began to use it together. The abuse got worse, and the addiction got worse.

We ended up getting put out of the apartment because we weren't paying any bills, and we only managed to keep my car because my parents began to realize what was going on and would make the car payment so that I had transportation. I continued to work every day but would leave work, leaving my clients waiting while I used and came back. It was a vicious cycle.

Things got so bad that I figured I would repeat the process that helped me to get clean the last time. I thought, okay, let me move back home again and start this thing over. I went home and vowed to myself that I would never see him again and that this would be the last time. I held on for a while, but the using got worse. Instead of things getting better, it increased because I was so sad and depressed, and I started seeing him again. And we brought all of our destructive behavior to my parent's house, and they began to get involved.

I was driving back and forth daily to work in Rock Hill and getting paid just to use. I was out one day using and my mother came and got me. My mother rescued me. She was that shepherd who came to rescue her sheep. She came and took me to the emergency room, and in the emergency room, I told them what was going on, and they signed me up for an outpatient treatment center.

But that was not good for me. I needed to be inpatient. So I went to treatment for 30 days, away from everyone, but I still maintained conversations with the person that I was involved with. I shouldn't have done that because it kept me from concentrating on my work in the program because we can be addicted to people, places, and things as well.

Once I got out of treatment, I went to a transitional home for 30 days, and it didn't work because I didn't stay clean. I went back to him, and the abuse and the drugs started again. As a result, I got kicked out of the transitional home, went back to my parent's house, and continued to use and see him, but I always went to my meetings because I believed if we got clean, everything would be okay, but that's just not how it worked. The abuse continued, and I can remember my father going after him with the gun because he had abused me. And it was by the grace of God that he saw my father, but my father didn't see him. I knew that somebody would get hurt if it didn't get better and do something different. By this time, I was tired, and it had gotten to the point that I wasn't afraid anymore. I began to carry sample cans of aerosol hairspray and a cigarette lighter, and I would tell myself that if he abused me, I was going to set him on fire.

I began to fight back because I was so tired. I was willing to go to jail if I had to kill him because I started to hate myself so much. I hated him, and I hated myself even more because I was not strong enough to walk away, and I began to realize this is how people have a nervous breakdown. My experience with domestic abuse gave me compassion for people who think about committing suicide. I never thought about committing suicide, but I thought about being able to escape somewhere so far away from everything that he couldn't find me.

I was addicted to this toxic relationship. I was addicted to my boyfriend, and I still didn't know how to let go. I was introduced to Narcotics Anonymous at the treatment center. One of the guidelines was to go to 30 meetings in 30 days. Take one day at a time. Get a sponsor. Work the program.

So I went to 30 meetings, and in 30 days, I found a sponsor. I found my first sponsor through the type of car she drove. I identified with the car. I had a Fiero. She had a Saab. I didn't do everything that was suggested for me because I kept going back to using. I had so many white chips that I could give out white chips when there was a meeting. The white chip is a chip of surrender. The white chip represented that I was tired of the life I was living, that I was tired of using. I'm ready to surrender. The white chip is the chip that we pick up if you have relapsed and a sign you're coming back. I'm surrendering all over again. And I kept going back. I kept going back, but I also kept coming back to surrender.

The last time I used with my boyfriend, I felt that it was a setup. It didn't matter whether it was or not, because I fell for it and I used, but I went to a meeting that same day. I remember the way that people looked at me with disgust and disdain. And they told me they were not giving me another white chip because they said I would eventually kill myself. One person who used to be at the meetings was named Elmer. He would always kiss us on the cheek. Elmer didn't kiss me that day. I felt so bad. All the people that I trusted no longer trusted me. Their look towards me in their eyes was enough for me to make that my last time using.

The last time I used it was January 22nd, 31 years ago. But I didn't let go of the toxic relationship. I continued to be abused until I got tired. I was clean and knew I couldn't get him clean. It was not my responsibility to get him clean. The last time that I allowed myself to be abused by him, we went out of town, and I went against everything that I felt inside of me to do. I knew I shouldn't have gone with him, which is why learning to trust the God in you is vital. He will use your conscience to guide and protect you, but if you resist the inner nudging that is trying to protect you, you are putting yourself in unnecessary danger.

Before we went out of town, I told him that if he abused me, it would be the last time. He did abuse me, and it was a complete 360 to the same way he abused me the first time. We went out for ice cream and walked downtown Charleston, laughing and playing. I felt so free and happy, and suddenly, everything changed just like that.

I saw his eyes change, and he badgered me back to Rock Hill until we pulled over on the side of the road and went down this exit. It was a dirt road, and the car was bumping and going up and down because he was driving so fast and erratic, and he just stopped, and he pulled me out of the car, and he threw me in the bushes, and he pinned me down. He held me down for what felt like a lifetime. I remember thinking, if I just can get home, Lord, just allow me to get home. I'll never go back again. And God allowed me to get home.

The next day, the owner of the salon I worked at called and told me that his sister had been killed, and her abuser had killed her. She had broken up with him. He wanted to talk to her, and she went back to him, and he strangled her, and the place where he strangled her was this obscured building that used to be a school, and people would go there to get high, and I can remember being at that school one night getting high. I remember him choking me there because we were fighting over drugs.

He told me every time he tried to think of his sister or visualize his sister's face, he would see mine. I went to her funeral. I saw her lying in that casket. And I just remember thinking how it could have been me. The only difference was that God showed me grace and allowed me to live. That was the last time. Reality smacked me in the face with the hard truth that awaited me if I continued to go back to that relationship.

It was enough for me to walk away. I had to set some boundaries and make some changes. I couldn't accept any phone calls. I remember this lady telling me, "It's okay to love him, but you can love him from afar. You have to act as though he's dead. You have to pretend that he doesn't exist. You have to stop taking his phone calls because if you continue to take the phone calls, it's going to be that one day that you're feeling sad, that you're feeling vulnerable, that you're missing them, and you're going to go back." I couldn't go back.

So, I did all the things that were suggested for me to do. I walked away from that relationship, but entered another relationship too soon, and I took the baggage with me. I didn't take time to heal, to love myself, or discover my true identity void of insecurity. Because years of insecurity, worthlessness, and low self-esteem don't just disappear overnight or because you leave a bad relationship. They don't leave until you heal and rediscover who you are.

I did give myself time, and when we go through these domestic violence relationships, and we are grateful and lucky enough, or blessed enough or brave enough to be able to walk away from them, we need to give ourselves time to heal. We need to allow ourselves to grieve the relationship and forgive ourselves for the things we allowed ourselves to go through, and give ourselves time to learn how to love, inspect, and analyze ourselves, to get to know ourselves so that we don't repeat the same actions in the next relationship. Or, like Erica Badu said, being the bag lady, bringing all that same baggage into the next relationship like I did. Although my relationship didn't work out, God gave me my daughter, which was the best thing that could have happened to me.

CHAPTER FOUR

# ASJA'

*"For all the things that God has brought me through, He was preparing me for a time such as this."*

—Gail Estella

Over time, God brought me through every single obstacle that I faced: domestic violence, insecurities, and abuse. He delivered me from each one. As my confidence in Him grew, my love and trust in Him grew. Everything I endured and overcame was preparing me for my daughter. God gave me my daughter for a short time, for only 21 years. And some of those years, she was sick, and some of those years weren't so good for us. But I was prepared. She would need to see me having a relationship with God because she would need her own relationship with God herself to go through the things that she did.

My daughter, Asja', was diagnosed with brain cancer in 2009 at the age of 13. We had to go to St. Jude Children's Research Hospital and found out that it was stage four Cancer. We went to St. Jude for a year. I can remember seeing my baby in the hospital bed after she was diagnosed with cancer and after her first surgery. I was asking God, why? "This is my only child. My finances are being attacked. My baby's health is being attacked. I don't understand what you're doing, God." And He told me to trust Him, and I did. I trusted God during our entire process at St. Jude, the good, the bad, and the ugly. I trusted him because I knew he would bring us through it.

Have you ever been in an unfavorable situation, but you had peace, calmness, or something that you can't even understand or really explain? That's what I experienced. We needed our faith because we were surrounded by children who were fighting for their lives; we watched people with whom we had forged relationships die. But we knew that we had to trust God. It was short-lived, and something would come out of the situation that would help someone else. St. Jude had a certified school there, and Asja' was determined to graduate from her class of 2013.

Her school would send their classwork, which she would complete. She would even do her schoolwork while she was undergoing chemotherapy treatments. She was determined, resilient, and persistent and had childlike faith. She just knew that God would heal her, and He did. We came home, and life was good. Everything that the devil tried to take away, God gave back to Asja'. The doctor said that she would have to attend remedial classes because of her cognitive issues. God didn't let that happen. God allowed her to graduate from high school with a 4.25 GPA.

In all of this, I wasn't aware that God was still preparing me for something else that was going to happen. God was strengthening me. God was strengthening my relationship with Him, and my faith grew because I witnessed what He had done. We knew who God was and what He could do. We knew God was a healer and a way-maker. We knew God was a provider because we watched Him provide for us. We didn't allow us to lose anything. God allowed me to return to work, and 90% of my clientele stayed with me. He sustained us mentally, physically, and spiritually. But I couldn't go back to the relationship that I was in. I tried, but I couldn't continue cohabitating with someone who wasn't going to marry me. God had done so much for me, and for me to continue the same lifestyle that I had before would be like a slap in God's face. And I couldn't do that.

By now, some of my insecurities were no longer plaguing me. I was feeling strong and feeling better about myself. I had a chance to be with me for the first time in years. Even though it was in an ugly environment, in a bad situation, it was beautiful at the same time. Asia continued to flourish. Things didn't come as easy for her in high school and college, but she worked for it. Friends didn't come as easy for her, but unlike me, she believed in herself. Asja' had an area in the back of her head where her hair was thin because of her chemotherapy. I had insecurities about her hair thinning. I wondered if people would accept her if boys would like her. I was projecting my 11-year-old self onto my daughter, but she didn't allow it to happen, and I thank God for that. I often tell her and God how sorry I am for projecting my insecurities on her and ask for forgiveness.

Taking ownership of who you are is taking accountability when you realize that your mind-sets and habits impacted or could impact someone negatively. Always be quick to apologize and take part in your role in influencing or affecting others. Accountability keeps your heart pure and lets others know that you are aware that you are a work in progress in that area.

Thank God my daughter had high self-esteem and was secure in who God created her to be. Because of that, she continued to prosper and excel and even made the dean's list in college. Asja' majored in speech pathology but didn't get a chance to continue her schooling there because she got sick again and had to come home. I remember her calling her father because she had a feeling in her throat, and it ended up being a pneumothorax. A pneumothorax is a collapsed lung. Her collapsed lung never fully healed, and the doctors believed it may have been because of the high dosage of radiation and chemo to her brain and spine, which affected her lungs.

It was a short-lived illness, and I'm so glad that God didn't allow Asja' to suffer. We still trusted that God was going to heal her because we had seen her healed from cancer, so we knew he could heal her from this. We knew this was a small matter for God, but he had a different plan. On June the 29th, 2019, Asja' passed. People kept asking me if I was okay and if I felt like going back to using cocaine. I always thought that if anything could take me back to using or cause me to relapse, it would be the death of my daughter, my one and only daughter. She had grown to be my best friend. But It didn't cross my mind to use because God had brought me so far and prepared me spiritually for her death.

I knew that going back to using would be dishonoring God because of all the things that he had done and dishonoring Asja' because she had persevered through so much. She had shown such perseverance and childlike faith through her illness that I would not disrespect her and turn back to drugs. I also knew that if I used this time, I was going to die, if not a physical death, then surely a spiritual one. I couldn't escape the pain by getting high. I had to feel the pain of her death and her not being here with me. I had to feel the hurt of that hurt.

I remember someone telling me that it was okay to feel pain, that it wasn't going to kill me, and I had to feel it. I felt the pain alright. There were days that I could not get out of bed because I hurt so badly. There were days that I could not take a shower. Asja's voice would echo, "Get up dirty butt. Go take a shower. Get up and put some clothes on." And I did because I also knew that if I stayed in that down place, I would sink so far that I wouldn't have the energy to climb back out. So, I put my feelings aside and trusted God with yet another challenging and painful process.

Asja's funeral was on a Wednesday, and I went back to church that following Sunday because I worked with the youth and I couldn't stay away from God. I also went to therapy, and I stayed in therapy for four years. I shared my feelings without shame, and all this time, God was still birthing something inside of me. I didn't understand what it was at the time. Asja's death was rebirthing me. It brought life back to me because I knew that she served her purpose and was with God. I had taken care of her, and it was my time. I had given up so much for her, as we parents often do, and now it was my turn to take care of myself.

Now was my time to feed and love that little 11-year-old girl in me and to learn to live again. Now was my chance to do things that I had dreamt of and that I didn't have the confidence to do before. If you are willing to discover the source of your insecurity and go through the process of healing and transformation, I believe now can be your chance, too.

*"Feeling 'not good enough' is a common emotional battle. But remember, feelings are products of thoughts and emotions, and you have the power to conquer them."*

—*Omar Shariff*

𝓘've overcome the deep struggles of domestic violence and drug addiction, and through that journey, I've come to grasp how powerful insecurity can be. However, I want you to know there is hope. You hold the strength within yourself to conquer insecurity. In my journey to wholeness, I have found the following keys to overcoming insecurity and walking in your true, authentic greatness.

## Identifying our Insecurities

By identifying when our behaviors are just compensations for insecurities, we can seek out our true, authentic selves. For me, I learned to be okay with being alone. I'm an introvert. I prefer my personal space and time. I accepted myself for who I was, and by accepting myself, I began to like myself. I didn't need to be at every event and be friends with everyone anymore because I liked the person I was with–me.

Understanding our insecurities is the very first and crucial step towards conquering them. Insecurity can be sly and tricky, often pretending to be a way to protect ourselves. Because of these hidden fears, we might feel hesitant about trying new things, fearing we might end up embarrassed. It's like our minds are playing a sneaky game, making us believe we're keeping safe when we're just holding ourselves back. It's important to know that even those who seem super confident on the outside may struggle with their own insecurities.

We gain the power to overcome these hidden insecurities once we shine a light on them. It's like turning on a light in a dark room—the more we know about our insecurities, the less control they have over us. This profound realization has been a game-changer in my journey towards discovering who I am and growing as a person.

## Acknowledge the Source of Your Insecurities

Understanding and addressing our insecurities is crucial to personal growth and well-being. It means digging into the origins of these feelings, recognizing the experiences or situations that have contributed to them, and taking proactive steps toward self-improvement.

When you think about what makes you feel insecure, consider different parts of your life that might have influenced it. This could be experiences with friends, how your family interacts, or even the pressures society puts on you. These things could have impacted how you see yourself and your relationships. By untangling these thoughts and experiences, you gain essential insights into your insecurities, which helps open the path for personal growth and healing. Remember, this journey of understanding yourself is vital to gaining confidence.

As I look back on this journey, it's clear that embracing our insecurities and understanding their roots is a powerful step towards building healthier relationships with others and ourselves. It's a process that takes time and kindness.

Through this introspection, true growth and self-assurance find their way.

Venturing forward on this path towards self-improvement, I am mindful of its significance. It's a transformative journey, leading towards a deeper sense of self-worth and a stronger ability to connect meaningfully with others. With each step, I am reminded that understanding and addressing insecurities is not just about self-preservation but a powerful stride toward a more fulfilling and enriched life.

Overcoming your insecurities is a process. It will take time, effort, and intentionality. You will have victories and setbacks. I can tell you first-hand that it will be a challenge, but it will be worth it.

**Here are some steps you can take to help you overcome insecurity:**

**Resist your natural thinking process.**

Have you ever heard the saying, "To get something you have never had, you have to do something you have never done." Well, that same thinking process applies to overcoming insecurities. To overcome insecurity, you must think like you've never thought before. Our insecurities are a part of our innate defensive mechanism.

It is our natural way of protecting ourselves from things that make us uncomfortable. However, it becomes toxic when it leads us to distrust, dislike, fear, and avoidance of the world around us. To break our insecurities' control, we must resist our natural inclination to feel the emotion of insecurity.

That means you will still feel the emotion, but you must resist it and move forward in the opposite direction. This looks different for each person. As I said, I displayed insecurity by being present for every event and trying to be friends with everyone. Resisting my natural inclination looks like *not* attending the event where all my friends will attend.

I understand that my friends will not talk negatively about me when I'm not around, and I am okay with the possibility that they might. For someone else, it may mean resisting the urge to dislike someone because they are successful or attractive and understanding that their success or beauty does not reflect upon you.

## Give Yourself Grace

For all of us, no matter our insecurities, it will mean looking at the man or woman we see in the mirror and learning to like and love that person. Our insecurities represent what we don't like about ourselves because, at some point, life experiences, people, or media made us feel that something about us was wrong, imperfect, or undesirable.

However, when you love yourself unconditionally, you will give yourself grace to be who you are—authentic–flaws and all. Think about a mother's love for her newborn baby. The mother does not reject the baby when he/she soils his/her diaper. The mother does not shame the baby while he/she is learning to walk and falls or when the baby mispronounces words. The mother gives the baby grace to grow.

It's okay to make mistakes and face challenges. These experiences are a natural part of growing and learning. They don't define your worth or abilities. By facing them head-on, you build resilience and confidence in yourself. On this journey called life, you will not always get it right. You will not be the best-looking, the smartest, or the wealthiest person. You will never be able to please everyone or be liked by everyone. You must give yourself the grace to be perfectly imperfect. You must love yourself enough to handle the hate of the entire world if need be.

## Walk Away from Toxic Relationships

It's important to realize that feeling insecure is like a seed. Suppose we keep giving it attention and care. In that case, it can grow more prominent, which means there might be specific places, situations, or people in our lives that unknowingly worsen our insecurity. Sometimes, we think these people are kind and supportive because they're paying attention to us, but they make us feel more insecure.

Recognizing these sources of ongoing insecurity is a big step in breaking free from them. It means noticing the patterns and connections between specific situations, places, and people that consistently make us doubt ourselves. It also means separating from people who make us feel good about our insecure behaviors. Friends who encourage us to hate others do not help us; they enable our insecure behavior.

When we understand these things, we can start taking action to reduce their impact and build a more positive image of ourselves. It's good to know that overcoming insecurity is a journey that takes time and patience. It involves becoming more aware of ourselves and learning to tell the difference between things that are good for us and things that aren't.

Remember, you have the power to change how you feel about yourself. Insecurities are no more than thoughts. They have no power. You can change them by resisting your natural thinking habits, giving yourself grace, spending time with those who make you feel good, and spending time in places that help you grow and feel positive. With determination and kindness, you can gradually replace insecurity with confidence and love the person you see in the mirror.

# CHAPTER SIX

# FROM INSECURE TO SECURE

*"Therefore if any man be in Christ, he is a new creature: old things are passed away; behold, all things have become new.*

*—2 Corinthians 5:1*

$\mathcal{G}$oing from insecure to secure is a process that causes us to go through different stages to become the person God created us to be. This process is an eternal and external metamorphosis similar to the transformative experience of a caterpillar to a butterfly.

I've talked about my insecurities. We've gone through domestic violence, the substance abuse, the loss of my daughter, and even how to identify and prevent insecurity so you don't have to go down some of the same paths that I did. Now, we're going to talk about the butterfly. My logo is the butterfly, and I chose it because it goes through metamorphosis. It goes through four stages, but we're going to talk about the three stages of the butterfly. The first stage is the caterpillar.

The caterpillar is the most vulnerable stage of the butterfly, where people walk past, kick, and step on the caterpillar. If you remember, as a kid, you might have put the caterpillar in a jar and then cut holes in it just to see how long it would live. This is the most vulnerable stage of the caterpillar, but the caterpillar is destined to become a butterfly if it lives and goes through the stages. The caterpillar is the stage where the insecurities take place, when you don't feel you're pretty enough, or you may feel you're too pretty. You may feel your hair should be shorter or longer. You're too light, you're too dark, you're too tall, you're too short, you're too thin, you're too fat, you're uncomfortable with yourself. You're just aimlessly crawling around because you need to figure out who you are, what you are, or where you are going. At this stage, you allow anything to happen to you and accept anything because you're not confident enough to stand up for yourself. You're not confident enough to believe in yourself. You're not confident enough to know who you are. So you're still the caterpillar.

The caterpillar stage represents a pivotal juncture where many find themselves teetering on the precipice of addiction, unsure if they've already crossed the threshold. They cling to the illusion of control, believing they can put a halt to their dependency, only to discover the grip of addiction tightening with each unsuccessful attempt to resist.

In the depths of an abusive relationship, denial overshadows reality, obscuring the truth of its toxicity, leaving victims to question their worth and their actions, desperately seeking a reason for the abuse inflicted upon them by those they love. They convince themselves that altering their behavior or appearance may put a stop to the violence, but they instead remain trapped in a cycle of self-blame and helplessness.

You can also experience grief in the caterpillar phase, which can result from a lost life or a lost relationship. This can be a family member or a friend, so someone important or impacting your life. Grief can prompt introspection laced with regret and what-ifs. People replay moments in their minds, grappling with perceived missed opportunities, wondering if different words or actions could have altered the course of their fate.

In my case, sometimes I think I might have pushed my daughter too hard. I began to question myself. Did I push her too hard? But I do know now that if I hadn't pushed her, she wouldn't have achieved many things that she accomplished. But I often wondered if she knew I loved her as much as I did. Did she know that I would've gone through heaven and hell for her? And I did. And did she know that she was the most important person in my life? And sometimes I ask God, did I love her too much? Did I put her before you? Was her death some type of punishment for me?

But thank God that He sees us crawling around aimlessly. He saw me crawling around, picked me up, and put me in this cocoon. The technical name for the cocoon for a caterpillar or butterfly is chrysalis. He puts us in this chrysalis, wraps us up tightly, and turns us upside down. We will be uncomfortable in this stage because this is where the metamorphosis takes place, where God is changing and evolving you. God is taking you from a caterpillar and preparing you to become a butterfly.

In this stage, you have acceptance of who you are. God establishes you in the truth of your identity, that you are fearfully and wonderfully made, that He made you unique, and teaches you how to love yourself. The cocoon is also the stage of acceptance, acknowledging where you are, whether it be abuse or addiction, but understanding that He is giving you the grace and the tools to walk away from it. In becoming the butterfly, you recognize your worth, that you deserve better than this, that you are better than this, and that you don't have to allow a person to hit you or verbally abuse you. You don't have to allow a person to abuse you emotionally, sexually, psychologically, or financially.

In the cocoon stage, God can reassure you that His strength in you is enough. He is dealing with your heart and allowing you to see yourself. In this stage, I had to come to terms with the fact that I was an addict, and to deny that truth would also be denying the help that I needed the help in the first place. It was in the cocoon that I was finally able to say, "My name is Gail, and I am an addict." It was a period of self-awareness and acceptance that I made different choices and couldn't just do anything or go anywhere because influences affected me differently than others. It's a season that requires you to be present, taking one day at a time and not venturing too far into the future's what-ifs.

I had to learn to trust God, knowing that He was molding me and that the desire would go away in time. In time, that drug will not be the first thing you run to. You're going to run to God first and eventually be able to stand up in front of others and tell them how God brought you through, sharing with them that you do not have to pick up today, that you do not have to use today, and that there is an alternative way of life.

The cocoon stage is not only an acceptance of yourself but also an acceptance of others that you had to walk away from on your journey of transformation. Accept that you did all you knew how to do at the time. You won't continue to question life with regrets, questioning your ac-

tions and whether or not you could have done
more. You find forgiveness and acceptance for
yourself and others, understanding that God is in
control and that He alone knows the outcome.
But the great thing about God is that He heals the
brokenhearted and helps them to love again. You
don't have to be burdened with guilt and con-
demnation. You will be able to smile again.

But you must allow God to heal you from the
hurt and the pain. He's preparing you to be able
to love yourself because you feel so bad, guilty,
and ashamed for some of the things you've done
and places where these things took you. But
God's saying," You don't have to be embarrassed
anymore. You don't have to allow yourself to be
in bondage. You can be set free." God has been
preparing you for a life of freedom in the cocoon
stage, and it could take anywhere from two
weeks up to two years, depending on how
yielded you are to God's work.

God might have to protect you a little longer.
God might have to wrap himself around you a
little tighter than others. But it's okay because we
all are different, and God knows what each of us

requires based on what we have been through and the level of hurt and pain we have experienced.

The cocoon stage is about allowing God to teach you how to stay in your lane with blinders. When God is doing a work in you, you must remain focused on Him without looking to the left or right to see what the next person is doing and how they're doing it. This stage is all about you, all about you. God is preparing you and equipping you to become someone more beautiful than you ever imagined, and it's more than an external appearance. It will be an inner freedom and metamorphosis that will cause you to become unrecognizable to others.

God is giving you a newfound confidence that even if you had it, After being a victim and giving your power away, God is now giving you your power back. God allows you to laugh, smile, look at yourself in the mirror, and like what you see without shame. You are stronger now. You're not that caterpillar anymore. After God has molded you and taken you through this metamorphosis, God has changed you, equipped you, and allowed you to become that butterfly.

Once you become the butterfly, God allows all the wrappings to dissipate as you adjust to having wings. Moving from a caterpillar in a cocoon to a butterfly can be challenging. The presence of wings implies that you are ready to fly, but whether or not you can take off is up to you. Although you are now different, if you take off in flight too fast, the new environment can cause you to want to retreat to the caterpillar stage where you were just aimlessly crawling around because you're not entirely sure of how to fly and adjust to being a butterfly in a new environment. Although you have changed, you may still be used to life on the ground. But God will guide you, direct you, and show you the way so you can fly.

When you think about the butterfly, it flies with the wind; it doesn't fly against the wind. So God has allowed you to fly and is carrying you now, but you have to allow yourself to be carried. You must allow yourself to be this new creature, understanding that you are no longer the same. The butterfly is not as quickly captured as the caterpillar was. It's not hanging upside down in the same vulnerable state as the cocoon. To capture a butterfly, you must have this long handle with a net. It won't be easy to capture and take advantage of you anymore. People are going to have to look at you differently. People will have to respect you and treat you differently because you are different.

As you fly with the wind, allow God to take you wherever He'll have you to be. It may be frightening, and you might be nervous and fearful about where you may land, but you have to trust God through the process and remember that God has brought you through being a caterpillar and being in the cocoon. He has brought you through a complete metamorphosis. So look at yourself in the mirror; look at your wings. Imagine any color you want them to be. Just close your eyes, think about what color your wings are, and imagine flying in the freedom of your new identity as God carries you to your destination. He's carrying you to your next, to be the person you were always destined to be.

Remember, the caterpillar was always destined to become a butterfly. So, allow yourself to be the bold, beautiful butterfly that you are. Allow yourself to love yourself again and to respect yourself because you deserve it. Regardless of how traumatic or painful, everything you went through was for a purpose: to tell another person about what God has brought you through so that they, too, can emerge the butterfly they were always destined to be. So walk with your head held high and shoulders back because you know who you are now. You're a new creature, and all old things have passed away. You're this new, beautiful butterfly, and now it's your time to fly. Fly, my beautiful butterfly. This is who you are now-a bold, beautiful butterfly. Fly, fly, fly, fly, fly....

# Notes

# Notes